RAILS ACROSS BRITAIN

THIRTY YEARS OF CHANGE AND COLOUR

RAILS ACROSS BRITAIN

THIRTY YEARS OF CHANGE AND COLOUR

DAVID CABLE

PEN & SWORD
TRANSPORT

First published in Great Britain in 2017 by
Pen & Sword Transport
An imprint of Pen & Sword Books Ltd
47 Church Street
Barnsley
South Yorkshire
S70 2AS

ISBN 9781473849136

Printed and bound by Replika Press Pvt. Ltd.

Pen & Sword Books Ltd incorporates the imprints of Pen & Sword Archaeology, Atlas, Aviation, Battleground, Discovery, Family History, History, Maritime, Military, Naval, Politics, Railways, Select, Social History, Transport, True Crime, and Claymore Press, Frontline Books, Leo Cooper, Praetorian Press, Remember When, Seaforth Publishing and Wharncliffe.

For a complete list of Pen & Sword titles please contact
Pen & Sword Books Limited
47 Church Street, Barnsley, South Yorkshire, S70 2AS, England
E-mail: enquiries@pen-and-sword.co.uk
Website: www.pen-and-sword.co.uk

DAVID CABLE – OTHER PUBLICATIONS

Railfreight in Colour (for the modeller and historian)

BR Passenger Sectors in Colour (for the modeller and historian)

Lost Liveries of Privatisation in Colour (for the modeller and historian)

Hydraulics in the West

The Blue Diesel Era

Rails Across North America – A Pictorial Journey Across the USA

Rails Across Canada – A Pictorial Journey Across Canada

Rails Across Australia – A Journey Through the Continent

Rails Across Europe – Northern and Western Europe

Rails Across Europe – Eastern and Southern Europe

Introduction

Rails Across Britain is a photographic album showing virtually all the trains that have operated on the main lines of Great Britain since the mid-1980s to the present day. The book makes reference to Metro train systems, part of which operate on (ex) National Rail tracks (Transport for London, Docklands Light Railway and Tyne & Wear Metro), but excludes tramways, preserved railways and track maintenance equipment, all of which justify books in their own right. Passing reference is made to steam trains operating on the main lines.

The decades that have passed in the thirty year period have, perhaps, seen some of the most dramatic changes to the British Railways system since its inception in the nineteenth century. Not only has the previous state owned British Rail network been 'sold' off to the private sector as far as train operations are concerned (although the funding of track maintenance and development has remained virtually on the government's books), but a substantial change in the types of trains used has taken place.

It was in the mid-1980s that significant structural changes took place within British Rail, under the auspices of Chairman Sir Robert Reid and his successor, Sir Bob Reid. Up until then, BR had worked as a corporate monolith, but it was under these gentlemen that cost centres and control systems were introduced. Although there had been two 'deviations' from the blue and grey corporate identity – Scotrail and InterCity – these were basically cosmetic. The cost centre regime established separate identities and responsibilities for the different operating elements of BR, namely InterCity, Network South East, Regional Railways, Parcels (later Rail Express Systems) and Railfreight. The latter was further subdivided into Coal, Construction, Metals, Petroleum and Railfreight Distribution (RFD), later becoming Trainload Freight divided into Loadhaul, Mainline, Transrail and Railfreight Distribution, reflecting geographical areas rather than commodities. All of these different sectors carried their own liveries or decals, making a welcome change from the all-pervading BR blue era.

At the outset of this period, there were still many locomotives and multiple units emanating from the 1955 modernisation programme, supplemented by more up-to-date designs from the 1960s and 1970s. But none of these performed to the levels achieved in the twenty-first century. Compared with the present day, there were many more locomotive hauled passenger trains and more frequent freight services whilst industry was still relatively buoyant. It is salutary to reflect on how these numbers have changed over the years. From 1966 to 2015 there has been a 67 per cent reduction in the number of locomotive classes, but only a 25 per cent reduction in multiple units.

In the mid-1990s, the Tory government introduced legislation to privatise the railways, franchised Train Operating Companies

(TOCs) working the trains, Rolling Stock Leasing Companies (ROSCOs) providing the rolling stock, and Railtrack/Network Rail maintaining and developing the tracks and infrastructure. The result was a massive change from the financial restrictions imposed by the Treasury on the nationalised BR system, to a surprisingly large level of financial input now funded by the State, and an explosion of colour schemes, some tasteful and others appalling. During the privatisation era, there were many changes in the franchised operators, resulting in new colour schemes (which all have to be paid for by the travelling public) and the demands of the Treasury for the franchisees to pay back premium emoluments.

Whether privatisation has been beneficial is open to conjecture, although the fact remains that passenger numbers have increased dramatically throughout this period. Correspondingly the numbers of freight trains has reduced, especially those handling coal, but instead of many wagon load services in previous years, freight trains are now almost exclusively formed in block loads.

The inconsistent performance of rolling stock, particularly of locomotives, and the dearth of orders for new stock prior to privatisation, resulted in new generations of trains being introduced, although this had been presaged by the acquisition and remarkable performance of EMD built locomotives from 1986 by the stone handling companies in the Mendips – Yeoman and ARC – and later National Power in Yorkshire. The Trainload Freight and RFD activities had been taken over by Wisconsin Central, whose disgust at the performance of the British Class 47s resulted in them placing an order for 250 up-to-date EMD built locos, the Class 66, which transformed the reliability of the company's locomotive fleet. In turn, Bombardier in particular introduced new and more reliable multiple units, both diesel and electric, in their Turbostar and Electrostar ranges, and these developments have led to more innovative designs over the intervening years, such as the Class 700 Thameslink EMUs and the Class 800 IEP sets.

Considering the current designs of rolling stock, what is apparent is how better safety is ensured through the abandoning of slam door coaching stock in favour of sliding door vehicles that most main line passenger services have dispensed with locomotives in order to reduce turnaround times at termini, and that the use of block loads for freight trains has virtually eliminated (re-) marshalling of wagons serving local sidings, which themselves have also largely disappeared. However, the widespread use of fixed multiple unit formations has left no flexibility to meet particular events (e.g. Rugby matches, exhibitions etc), apart from a limited level of service provided by non-franchised private operators such as West Coast Railways.

So this book of around 200 photographs portrays the scene over the last thirty years, during which time many locations were more accessible, with the restrictions of tree growth etc, the range of rolling stock designs changed markedly, and the myriad of colour schemes brightened up the surroundings, even though the variety of classes became more repetitive. The photographs are all of my own taking, a few having been used by Colour Rail in the past. They are shown in the order of taking the shots and where more than one photo of a particular class is shown, it will be in a different colour scheme. The photos have been taken during days out, on holidays and during work away from home, and cover from Scotland to Cornwall, and East Anglia to North Wales. The book provides a comprehensive coverage of almost all the classes that have worked on BR and the privatised railways over this thirty year period.

David Cable
Hartley Wintney, Hants
August 2015

On a humid evening in July 1985, a pair of 4CAP units, 413308 trailing, pass Hoo Junction on their way from Charing Cross to Gillingham. A Class 33 lurks in the siding ready to haul a Willesden bound Speedlink service. Class 413 4CAPs were formed of two Class 414 2 HAPs.

A Plymouth to Paddington express sweeps through Aldermaston station in August 1985, behind a sparkling Class 50 50045 *Achilles*. Note the head shunt for the long-gone Padworth sidings.

Class 25 25265 moves steadily northwards through Chesterfield, with a mixed set of empty Mark 1 and Mark 2C coaches in October 1985.

Class 45 45040 has been given the road to leave the Kings Lynn dock line with its train of empty hoppers. The approach to the station is seen on the left. Taken in January 1986.

InterCity livery has now started to become more widespread as shown on Class 87 87004 *Britannia* working a Liverpool Lime Street to Euston express in February 1986. With the industries of Warrington discernible in the murky background, the train has just passed over the Manchester Ship Canal Bridge at Moore.

The class leader (if you can call it that, since there were only two of them!) Class 151 151001 leaves Derby for Matlock in March 1986, as the prototype Class 150 (150001) arrives with the return service. I always thought what a stylish deign the Class 151 was, and never heard any adverse comments about them. But I suppose BR Workshops wanted the Class 150, rather than give work to Metro Cammell, who produced the Class 151. Such is politics.

Hastings Class 201 DEMU 1006 pounds its way up the bank from Tonbridge and approaches the tunnel at Polhill in March 1986. It leads another set, forming a Hastings to Cannon Street service. The Hastings line was one of the first diesel worked passenger lines in the UK, using the thin profile units designed specifically for this section.

Transferred from Scotland, and now carrying Manchester PTE orange and brown colours, Class 303 303067 stands in Manchester Piccadilly station having arrived with a service from Crewe. This unit has the modified front cab windows. Taken in April 1986.

In the original white and green colours for the Class 141, a Leeds to York service via Harrogate sweeps round the curves at Poppleton Junction, with a nice array of tracks and signals to add to this April 1986 view.

In the era before the old blue and grey was completely replaced by the new InterCity colours, with the church and houses of Dunbar peering over the fields, an Edinburgh to King's Cross High Speed Train (HST) passes, headed by Class 43 power car 43095. Taken on a glorious spring day in April 1986.

An unidentified Class 27 passes Saughton Junction in May 1986, working a short Edinburgh to Dundee service. The spires of Edinburgh highlight the background.

In the days when special trains were run for a variety of activities, the Football Cup Final at Wembley always attracted a number of extras. The 1986 match between Everton and Liverpool yielded several trains of enthusiasts, such as this all first-class train passing Hatch End behind a Class 81 electric loco.

The Jaffa Cake livery, adopted by London and South East, prior to Network South East always appealed to me. With Essex Express branding, Class 309 309605 brings up the rear of a Liverpool Street to Clacton train, seen leaving Colchester in May 1986.

Class 03 03089 sits quietly with its match wagon at March shed in May 1986. The match wagon is attached because the locomotive on its own is too short to guarantee being detected by track circuits.

Another class to carry Jaffa Cake colours was the Class 411. Unit 1600 has just exited Polhill tunnel and starts the downhill run through the verdant English countryside to Tonbridge in July 1986. The train is a Charing Cross to Hastings service.

One of the two experimental Class 210 DEMUs accelerates out of Newbury Racecourse station in July 1986. Four-car set 210001 is working a Reading to Bedwyn stopping train – the other set, 210002, was a three-car unit.

Class 85 85003 stops at Birmingham International station on its way from Euston to Birmingham New Street. It is August 1986, and the driver keeps a watchful eye on me!

Pride of the South Western lines, Class 432 2006 accelerates a Waterloo to Weymouth express out of Brockenhurst in September 1986. The 4REP uses its 3,000 horse power to propel a pair of 4TC trailer units. The Lymington branch is on the inside.

Converted from the passenger DMUs used on services out of St Pancras prior to electrification, Class 127 910 two-car parcels unit makes a smoky southbound exit from Bletchley, passing under the flyover. March 1987.

On a damp May day in 1987, Strathclyde PTE Class 318 318254 departs from Irvine, on its way from Glasgow Central to Ayr. A Class 08 hides behind the signal.

Strathclyde Class 314 set 202 leaves Uddingston on its way to Lanark in March 1987, under the careful eye of the man in the orange vest. Pity about the mast in the foreground. Why do they have to put them in the way of a photo?!

The leaves have yet to develop on the trees at Crowthorne in April 1987, where Class 319 L588 heads away from the station, working a Reading to Gatwick Airport service.

One of the Scottish DMUs, a Class 107 number 444, moves gently out of the bay platforms at Dundee to make its way to Perth, as indicated by the letter on the signal. Taken in May 1987.

A Class 110 DMU, working from Sheffield to York, passes the now-closed station at Rotherham Masborough in June 1987. This class was predominant in Yorkshire.

Carrying its Great Western green livery celebrating the composer, Class 50 50007 *Sir Edward Elgar* takes the through road at Tisbury loop and slows for the station stop. The date is June 1987, the train being a Waterloo to Exeter St Davids express. Note the mixture of NSE and Blue and Grey stock.

In fresh Railfreight Red Stripe colours, Class 31 31263 passes through Grantham with a northbound test train, heading, presumably, to Doncaster. A Class 150 awaits departure for Nottingham in the adjoining platform in August 1987.

A Network South East liveried Class 117 stops at North Camp in September 1987. The set is L411, working from Gatwick Airport to Reading. The Blackwater Valley dual carriageway overbridge now dominates the background.

The Basingstoke 150 celebrations in September 1987 produced a wealth of unusual static exhibits, but the shuttle service between Basingstoke and Ludgershall also provided a treat with D200 working one of the train sets. The green Class 40 is seen at Worting Junction with an appropriate maroon set of coaches, marred, of course, by the yobs in the front coach.

The West Midlands PTE painted one EMU in their canary yellow and light blue colours as used on their buses. It did not suit a train, as is illustrated by Class 312 312204, seen at Bescot in February 1988, working from Birmingham New Street to Walsall.

One of the Tyne & Wear PTE Pacers, Class 143 143023, leaves Thornaby on its journey from Darlington to Saltburn in February 1988. A Class 56 and Class 47 47301 wait for instructions.

Class 414 2HAP 4311 leads another 2HAP and a 4VEP past the carriage sheds at Farnham, in which another 4VEP lurks in the shadows. The train is an Alton to Waterloo semi-fast service, and was seen in September 1988.

On a November 1988 day devoid of colour, a Class 142 Pacer, in pseudo GWR chocolate and cream, crawls across the High Level Bridge at Newcastle, having commenced its journey in Middlesbrough. The colour scheme was introduced for these units when they were originally allocated to the West Country.

The March 1989 sun highlights the colours of a Class 114, decorated in Royal Mail colours. The set stands in a bay platform at the north end of Cambridge station, with a Class 101 alongside.

In the second version of Network South East colours, Class 50 50024 *Vanguard* approaches its destination, Paddington, with a service from Oxford. Seen in March 1989, an empty HST runs parallel ready to form an outbound service in due course.

With the oil seed rape coming into bloom, an unidentified Class 91 sprints south up the ECML near Offord in May 1989, propelling a Leeds to King's Cross express. Note the swallow emblem adjacent to the InterCity brand.

With a long way to reach its destination, DMU Class 156 156486 approaches Ely with an Ipswich to Blackpool service in May 1989. The spectacular array of signals here and in the distance at Ely Dock Junction, add to a pleasant evening's entertainment.

A portrait for the model makers shows the unique Class 89 89001 *Avocet* in full InterCity colours, on display at the Ilford depot open day in May 1989.

Standard WCML fare is seen at Dudley Port in June 1989, where Class 90 90019 is passing with a Glasgow to Penzance cross country service. Did anyone undertake the whole trip in one go?! One blue and grey coach mars the consist.

Over the years, Eastleigh depot has enhanced a few of its shunters in various colour schemes, but none as worthy as this. In full Southern Railway green, Class 08 08892 is just squeezed into the frame, as it sits in the works in September 1989.

The gorse is out in profusion near Inverkeithing, where a coal sector liveried Class 26 heads towards North Queensferry with a short ballast train. Taken in May 1989.

A parcels working enters the Brighton side of London Bridge in January 1990. The train comprises a Class 419 motor luggage van, number 9004, with a Class 416 2EPB.

The New Forest hosts a pair of Class 442 5WES EMUs, seen approaching Beaulieu Road station in August 1990, working a Waterloo to Poole service. As compared with other Southern Region units, which carried their set numbers on the front ends, these units only had them in the side banding, often making it impossible to identify the particular units when they travelled at line speed.

The Oxted line DEMUs of Class 207 tended to stay on their home territory, so to find one at Bramley working a Reading to Basingstoke train was a surprise. Class 207 207013 is seen leaving the station in September 1990, passing the abandoned sidings for the MOD depot in which I am standing.

Threading Carlyon Bay golf course is parcels liveried Class 47 47462 Cambridge T & RSD, which is working from Penzance to Paddington in November 1990.

Before being converted into two Class 153 single cars, Class 155 155324 passes Burngullow in November 1990 with a Penzance to Bristol working. The Parkandillack branch veers off round the bend.

Class 455 5834 exits Betchworth tunnel as it approaches Dorking with a Horsham to Victoria train in April 1991.

Seen at Luncarty in April 1991, Clas 47 47595 *Confederation of British Industry* heads south towards its next stop, Perth, with the well-loaded daytime Inverness to Euston express.

Passing an assortment of engineers' wagons at a location where expensive track work has now increased capacity and line speeds through the station, a Class 115 DMU approaches Princes Risborough station on its way from Marylebone to Banbury in April 1991.

Mainline coloured Class 37 37409 *Loch Awe* arrives at Fort William with the overnight sleeper service from Euston on a grey morning in June 1991. The Mainline description was used for locos that worked passenger services, but were not normally used on InterCity services, which were usually operated by engines with the brand name.

One did not normally expect to see a Scotrail liveried loco at Salisbury, but when the Class 47/7s were transferred to the Waterloo to Exeter services, such a sight could be seen for a short period before they were re-decked in NSE colours. In July 1991, 47704 *Dunedin* has arrived with empty stock from Eastleigh to form a service to Waterloo.

With the remains of St Catherine's Chapel on the hill, a diverted Southampton Docks to Waterloo boat train is seen between the tunnels south of Guildford station. The loco is Class 33 33102 and the date July 1991.

A Lincoln to Coventry service, worked by Class 150 150128, accelerates away from its starting point and passes East Holmes box, where semaphore signals still abound in March 1992. This unit is in the West Midlands colours.

A nice clean 'Bubble Car', Class 122 122112 stands on the stabling point at Exeter St Davids in April 1992. These units were originally introduced to replace steam operated Auto Trains on ex-Great Western branch lines.

Saturday extras and failures have led to Dutch liveried Class 33s being summoned for some mainline passenger services. 33035 passes Overton in April 1992 with a Waterloo to Exeter express, although whether it will arrive on time is open to speculation.

Class 114 set TO 72 passes Ancaster with its attractive Great Northern era signal box and station name board. The train is from Skegness to Nottingham, and the date is April 1992.

Having come down from Ludgershall and run round at Andover, Class 37 37278 starts away on its next leg to Dinton with an MOD service in June 1992. Note the coal sector decals on the engine.

Only two Class 33s were painted in NSE colours, 33035 and 33114. The latter named *Ashford 150* is seen at my local bridge, Potbridge, in June 1992, with a Waterloo to Exeter train, unusually on the down slow line and formed of InterCity coloured coaches.

West Yorkshire PTE Class 144 144020 is about to return from Knottingley to Wakefield in August 1992. Note the Class 08 in the sidings.

Strathclyde Class 320 320301 stands in Helensburgh station ready to depart for Airdrie in September 1992.

Nicely demonstrating Regional Rail colours, EMU Class 305 305506 is seen at Edinburgh with a train destined for North Berwick in September 1992. Note that the unit carries Scotrail branding instead of the normal Regional Railways. It is one of the units transferred from the GE/LTS lines.

Merseyside Class 507 507028 heads for the depot at Sandhills as another unit approaches in May 1993.

Class 73 Electro-Diesel 73138 speeds past Byfleet & New Haw in June 1993, with a Clapham Junction to Eastleigh driver training working. The train comprises a pair of Class 421 4CIG units.

Class 60 60006 *Great Gable*, carrying the correct Construction sector decals, passes the site of Helpston station as it takes the Stamford line with a Redland self-discharge train. The ECML is in the background. June 1993.

Pacer Class 143 143625 scurries along the down main line at Duffryn with a Gloucester to Cardiff train in July 1993. Basically, a Pacer is a bus body on four wheeels.

Metro Cammell Class 101 L835 enters Dorking West in June 1993, working a Reading to Gatwick Airport service. This station has been one of the least used on the British Railways system.

One Class 205 'Thumper' DEMU 205029 was restored to green colours, and in July 1993 is seen at Godstone with a Reigate to Tonbridge service, making a change from the standard NSE fare. This unit was destroyed in the head-on collision at Cowden on the Uckfield line in October 1994.

Part of the Tyne & Wear Metro system runs on what were BR tracks, as exemplified by this train – 4075 – calling for a lone passenger at Percy Main in September 1993.

Three Class 90s were painted in colours of European railways with which BR had close association. 90128 was painted in SNCB colours, 90130 in SNCF and 90129 in DB livery. The latter named *Frachtverbindungen* is seen on exhibition at Trafford Park in October 1993. The DB Red Bib Livery is slightly ruined by the mandatory BR yellow ends.

Over the years there have been a number of locos carrying non-standard colour schemes. One such was Class 31 31116 *Rail Celebrity* in the short-lived Infrastructure livery (47803 was the only other recipient). The Class 31 is grabbed at Crewe in January 1994, with a DVT and empty stock in tow.

Old Oak Common depot restored Class 47 47004 *Old Oak Common* TRSD to its original two-tone Class 47 colours. Seen in February 1994, it is passing Ruscombe with a down departmental working. Note the elm tree with the V-shaped top, a casualty of the 1987 hurricane, which has now regrown the missing branches.

A pair of Class 31s, 31270 and 31207, in coal sector and 'Dutch' colours, amble towards Winwick Junction with a short departmental working in February 1994.

Now branded with Gatwick Express decals and a light maroon stripe instead of standard InterCity colours, Class 73 73207 *County of East Sussex* propels a Gatwick Airport to Victoria train past the site of Coulsdon North. July 1994. The original SER lines via Redhill are hidden behind the undergrowth.

One of the very clean designed Class 323s arrives at Manchester Airport with a shuttle service from Manchester Piccadilly. 323225 carries the Manchester PTE colours and is seen in August 1994.

The autumn sun glints on the side of Loadhaul Class 56 56006, which is passing Burton Salmon with MGR empties bound for Gascoigne Wood, to collect another load of coal for one of the Aire Valley power stations. Taken in November 1994.

A Rugby to Crewe stopping service trundles past Slindon in April 1995, worked by an ex-GE/LTS Class 308 308134, repainted in to West Yorkshire PTE colours, but whether it will attract customers is another question.

Three car Class 323 323215 pulls to a stop at Longbridge with a Redditch to Litchfield service operated by West Midlands in April 1995.

The view from the road bridge at Acton Town in July 1995, shows the complex junctions, and captures two Piccadilly line trains, both working to and from Rayners Lane. July 1995.

Now carrying the smart Mainline blue colours, Class 73 73114 *Stewarts Lane* TMD heads east through Nutfield in October 1995, with the Bristol to Ashford vans, a type of train now no longer seen.

Preserved Class 71 electric loco E5001 was given a run out on the main lines in April 1996. With a Coventry to Eastbourne special in tow, it is seen on 3rd rail territory passing Farlington Junction.

National Power decided to invest in its own locomotives and rolling stock for transporting coal to its power stations in the Aire Valley. Class 59 59203 *Vale of Pickering* is seen with a loaded train from Gascoigne Wood passing Monk Fryston in July 1996. The locos have subsequently been taken over by EWS.

The grey version of Mainline livery did not appeal as much as the blue version, and on the egg-timer shape of the Class 58s could become very grubby. However, newly painted 58025 looks smart in the July 1996 sun, as it passes Stenson Junction with an MGR service.

Railtrack adopted a brown, white and grey colour scheme for its departmental locos and other powered stock. Bringing up the rear of a train to Tonbridge, ex-2HAP Class 414 EMU 930031 trails a mixture of coaches as it leaves Redhill in September 1996.

Units specifically devoted to working services between Liverpool Street and Stansted Airport were given a special livery. Class 322 322482 shows these colours off, as it wends its way through Bethnal Green in March 1997.

With the onset of privatisation, many new colour schemes came into existence. Connex took over South Central and South Eastern services at the outset, and Class 319 319217 (with a fellow unit) carry the yellow and white scheme, as they are seen passing Coulsdon North with a Victoria to Brighton express in March 1997.

The South West Trains modification to NSE colours of an orange stripe, is seen on Class 423 4VEP 3417, which pulls into Wokingham station with a Reading to Waterloo service in June 1997.

Mainline blue Class 58 58038 passes Denchworth in July 1997 with the Calvert to Avon 'Binliner'. The inability of a washing machine to clean the body side of this class between the cabs is amply demonstrated.

In July 1997, Class 55 Deltic D9000 *Royal Scots Grey* was given a test run prior to its being rostered to work a Saturday Ramsgate to Edinburgh service for a short summer period. In conjunction with Class 47 47827, it is seen near South Stoke in July 1997, hauling a morning Paddington to Manchester Piccadilly express, catching me completely unawares!

Transrail Class 60 60062 *Samuel Johnson* exits the Bishton flyover at Llandevenny with a pair of tanks being worked from Newport Alexandra Docks Junction to St Blazey. July 1997.

Two Class 60s, 60006 and 60033, were painted in British Steel blue, subsequently redone in Corus silver. 60033 *Tees Steel Express* negotiates Foxhall Junction and enters the balloon loop of Didcot power station to unload its load of coal, which it has brought up from Avonmouth in October 1997.

The attractive black and yellow Thameslink colours show up well in this February 1998 shot of Class 319 319448 leaving Radlett with a Luton to Brighton train. Note the banner signals for the junction ahead.

South West Trains Class 73 73109 *Battle of Britain* hauls NSE coloured Class 423 4VEP 3408 to Bournemouth depot in February 1998, and is seen from Campbell Road bridge at Eastleigh.

The new footbridge at North Camp allows a view of Virgin liveried Class 47 47807 about to pass the station on its way from Manchester to Brighton in April 1998. One of those useful cross country services that has been abandoned.

Class 86 86245 *Caledonian* was specially painted in colours reflecting its railway namesake. Heading towards Euston with an express from Wolverhampton, it is seen at Headstone Lane in May 1998, making a change from the standard Virgin red.

The standard Virgin format on the WCML is seen at Carpenders Park, where Class 87 87025 *County of Cheshire* (it should be *County of Chester* – Cheshire is itself a county name) heads north for Wolverhampton in May 1998. Oh, to have them again instead of Pendolinos!

The old Stansted Express Class 322s were acquired by the Northern franchise, which tried them out on services from Manchester Airport and Rochdale to Euston. The services didn't last long, but 322484 was seen in August 1998, working from Manchester Airport at Headstone Lane.

The one thing I did not expect to see at Carpenders Park was one of the North Of London Eurostar sets. However, Class 373 373301/2 worked down on a test trip in August 1998, making a significant change from the normal classes.

Great Western Trains were short of HSTs on some summer Saturdays, and borrowed sets from Midland Mainline and subsequently GNER. In the attractive teal green scheme, Class 43 43050 is seen at Cogload Junction in September 1998, working a Leeds to Newquay express.

The original green and ivory colours of Great West Trains show up nicely on a Paddington to Penzance HST, passing Creech St Michael in September 1998. Class 43 power car 43009 is in the lead.

Topped and tailed by Fragonset Class 31s, 31468 and 31452, a Bletchley to Bedford train, arrives at Bow Brickhill in September 1998. This two-coach train represents a good example of uneconomic working with two engines rostered just to avoid running round at each end, on a service ideally suited to a DMU.

The unique Class 89 89001 stands in King's Cross station, having arrived with an express from Leeds in June 1999. The gold GNER colours – the standard scheme – were replaced for a period, on this and a few other locos with a silver lettering version.

Before the Wessex franchise had decided on its corporate colour scheme, one Class 158 was decorated in this experimental scheme. 158867 is seen approaching Southampton Central with a Cardiff to Portsmouth Harbour service in August 1999. What a comedown on this service to have a two-car DMU in place of a five-coach train with a Class 33!

A classic view at Crofton, where ARC Class 59 59102 *Village of Chantry* takes the empties back from Theale to Merehead in August 1999. How much nicer this colour scheme was when compared to the current Hanson scheme.

A rare visitor to the Watford DC lines was seen in November 1999, when Railtrack Sandite 'Bubble' car Class 122 122019 ambled south at Headstone Lane.

At another location no longer available for photographers, Anglia Class 86 86235 *Crown Point* propels its Liverpool Street to Norwich express, past Pudding Mill Lane in November 1999.

For many years, the standard stock on the Watford DC lines, the North London and GN suburban services, were the Class 313s. Silverlink 313105 leaves Stonebridge Park in February 2000, with a Watford Junction to Euston train.

Regional Railways Class 37 37414 *Cathays C & W Works* stops at Caerphilly in February 2000, with a Rugby special from Rhymney to Cardiff. Note the non-standard coaching stock.

A North West Trains Class 150 works a Manchester Piccadilly to Llandudno train, passing Winwick Junction in June 2000. 150142 shows off its gold stars, even on a murky day such as this.

An Isle of Wight train from Shanklin approaches Ryde Pier Head in June 2000, wearing dinosaur livery – words fail me! Class 483 004 does the honours. This class replaced the original former London Transport standard stock introduced onto this line in 1967.

The first colours used on the newly franchised LTS lines were this white and green scheme, seen here on Electrostar Class 357 357015 leaving Limehouse on a down driver training run in July 2000.

Connex Class 456 456024 arrives at Purley in August 2000, working a Charing Cross to Tattenham Corner service. The unit is named *Sir Cosmo Bonsor*, and is seen passing Class 60 60096 *Ben Macdui*, which will leave for Cliffe presently.

Another special livery for Stansted Express units is carried by Class 317 317708, passing Bethnal Green with a down train from Liverpool Street in September 2000. Note the modified front end on these designated units.

The Bombardier Turbostar Class 170 DMUs were coming more and more into service by September 2000, as illustrated by 170109, working a Midland Mainline service from Nottingham to St Pancras passing West Hampstead. But a two-car DMU for a service between two major cities?

73128 was one of the only two Class 73s to carry EWS colours, and this has the original EW&S branding. It stands at the rear of a test train held at Clapham Junction in March 2001.

The MPV units have been used by Railtrack/Network Rail for various miscellaneous departmental duties. However, in August 2001, short-lived experiments were conducted to take containers from Willesden to Bulmers at Hereford, using MPVs DR98906/4. They are seen with four containers at Moreton, heading west.

One of the ROSCOs (Rolling stock leasing companies), Porterbrook, had five locomotives painted in their purple and white house colours. Re-engined and modified from a Class 47, Class 57 57601 passes Moreton with a Plymouth to Paddington via Bristol express in August 2001. Note Didcot Power Station in the background, in the days when coal fired plants still operated.

How nice the Thames Trains units looked in their blue, white and green colours, before the dreaded First group purple took over. Class 166 166217 heads west at Purley-on-Thames with a Paddington to Oxford semi-fast service in December 2001.

Another shot at Bethnal Green, now in January 2002, where Class 315 315861 works out to Chingford. It carries the West Anglia Great Northern deep purple colours, hardly the most inspiring choice for a train!

The Southern franchise, which replaced Connex South Central, painted some of its older stock with green ends and waist bands. Class 421 4CIG 1908 demonstrates this as it passes Millbrook in May 2002, with a now abandoned Victoria to Bournemouth train.

Thames Trains Class 165 165104 arrives at Newbury Racecourse station, with a Reading to Bedwyn stopping train in June 2002, with a surfeit of wild flowers on show.

Class 20 D8142 has been borrowed to help with wiring of HS1, and is seen with some curious wagons at Tut Hill in July 2002.

Towards the end of Virgin using Class 47s, a few were repainted into heritage and other colours. Resembling the original XP64 scheme, 47853 *Rail Express* passes Creech St Michael with a Paignton to Manchester express in July 2002.

LTS line Class 357 357205 carries c2c colours and branding, as it passes Shadwell DLR station on its way from Fenchurch Street to Shoeburyness in August 2002.

Another long gone service was the Anglia route from Basingstoke to East Anglia, using a circuitous and slow route via the North London lines. Passing Potbridge in August 2002, Class 170 170399 travels east on its way from Basingstoke to Chelmsford, making a change from standard SWT units.

Converted from a Class 416 2EPB unit, Railtrack Sandite unit 930002 has just passed Otford Junction, taking the Maidstone East line in October 2002. How did Railtrack financially justify a second colour scheme – what was wrong with the original?

Virgin Voyager Class 220 220001 *Maiden Voyager* passes Blackwater whilst working a Liverpool to Portsmouth Harbour cross country service in January 2003.

In the earlier part of the twenty-first century, the Docklands Light Railway made quite wide use of advertising on their units, until the latest corporate colours were introduced. DLR set 34 shows off the scheme portraying Maritime Greenwich, and is seen between West India Quay and Canary Wharf with a train to Lewisham. January 2003.

In Valley Lines colours, Pacer Class 142 142077 leaves Taffs Well for Coryton in February 2003.

The Valley Lines Class 150s carried advertising colours. Seen at Radyr on the same day, 150282 arrives with an Aberdare to Barry Island service.

Connex South East colours had been modified by March 2003, as seen at London Bridge on Class 466 466025 which is leading a Class 465 unit, working from Slade Green to Cannon Street.

Standard stock for diesel services operated by South West Trains is the Class 159. 159012 works a Salisbury to Waterloo semi-fast service, seen passing Berrylands in April 2003.

In the days when there were a few more international freight workings through the Channel Tunnel, Class 92 92015 *D.H. Lawrence* rounds the curve through Sandling station, with a Wembley to Dollands Moor service in May 2003. This class was equipped for both 25kV AC OHE and 750v DC 3rd rail power collection.

Some Class 319s carried this Good Days Out scheme, seen on 319218 about to stop at Kensington Olympia in July 2003. The service is from Watford Junction to Brighton, now modified to cover Milton Keynes to South Croydon.

Wessex Trains Class 158 158745 in the standard Wessex silver with maroon doors, passes Little Langford in the Wylye Valley, on its way from Cardiff to Portsmouth Harbour in August 2003. What a comedown from the days of a class 33 with five coaches, which used to operate these services.

Megapower of Classes 86 and 57 at South Kenton in September 2003, where Freightliner 86613, 86426 and 57005 accelerate away from Wembley with an Ipswich to Trafford Park intermodal working. However, the Class 57 was DIT (Dead in Transit).

Connex South East Class 365 365502 heads a Victoria to Ramsgate service and overtakes a very clean Class 423 4VEP, approaching Swanley Junction in September 2003. The Class 365s are now resident on outer suburban trains from King's Cross.

The all-pervading dreadful First group colours (my personal opinion, but shared by many) are carried by Class 175 175106, which is passing Abergele with a Manchester Piccadilly to Llandudno train in March 2004.

In the outer suburban blue version of South West Trains colours, an unidentified Class 450 heads east near Elvetham between Winchfield and Fleet, working a train from Basingstoke to Waterloo in May 2004.

In simplified One colours, Class 317 317729 hurtles past Broxbourne in August 2004, working from Stansted Airport to Liverpool Street.

On its last day of operation in December 2004, the loco topped and tailed train from Bristol to Brighton stops at Bradford-on-Avon. Matching the coaching stock pink, Class 31 31601 *Mayor of Casterbridge* brings up the rear of the train.

One of those treats, when a preserved loco takes to the main line, occurred in February 2005, when Class 52 D1015 *Western Champion* worked a special for retiring Bernard Staite. The Pullman train is passing Towney Crossing near Aldermaston on its way from Victoria to Taunton and Paignton, with the disused line to Padworth sidings in the foreground.

A pair of brand new Class 350s, unit 117 leading, arrive at Rugby on a driver training run from Bletchley in June 2005.

Heathrow Express operated Class 360 360202 pauses at Ealing Broadway with a Heathrow to Paddington stopping service in September 2005. There is a Central Line tube train in the bay platform alongside.

For a time, the North of London Eurostar sets were used by GNER on services between King's Cross and Leeds. Some, as in this instance, were repainted into GNER colours. Class 373 373305 *Yorkshire Forward* brings up the rear of an up service passing Alexandra Palace in November 2005.

Anglia Class 47 47714 struggles to get away from Colchester with a Liverpool Street to Norwich express in February 2006. The Class 90 at the rear of the train had failed, so the Class 47 undertook its 'Thunderbird' role.

Only one Class 59 was repainted into the very attractive Mendip Rail green, orange and grey colours. 59002 *Alan J. Day* passes Dean with a Whatley to Hamworthy stone train in April 2006.

Amongst its other purchases, Cotswold Rail (another short-lived enterprise) acquired two Class 87s, one of which, 87007, is seen at Carpenders Park running light engine in April 2006. This loco is now in Bulgaria.

One interesting working in May 2006 was the Class 325 Royal Mail EMUs, topped and tailed by Class 87s owned by First group, but previously DRS. With 87028 at the front and 87022 trailing, the three EMUs are seen passing Carpenders Park. The service was from Wembley Railnet to Shieldmuir.

The new broom has swept away the 5WES Wessex electrics, which have been replaced by the Siemens Class 444s. South West Trains' 444014 descends the bank from Buriton summit and is seen near Chalton in June 2006, with a Waterloo to Portsmouth Harbour express.

Five GBRF Class 66s were painted in Metronet colours, as seen on 66719, later named *Metro-Land*, which is working a Selby to Felixstowe intermodal service, passing Frinkley Crossing in August 2006.

Class 33 33103 *Swordfish* stands in Rugby station with the ex-SR General Managers saloon, an ex-Hastings line buffet car. The Fragonset-coloured engine will soon leave with a special working to Manchester. October 2006.

When taking photos at Berkeley Marsh, one expects to see Class 59s and stone trains, not West Coast Class 33 33029 hauling in-steam 4-6-0 850 *Lord Nelson*! The train was moving from Bishops Lydeard on the West Somerset to the East Lancs at Bury in November 2006.

Now in West Coast colours instead of the former Porterbrook purple and white, Class 57 57601 brings up the rear of a Waterloo to Yeovil Junction special. The train was hauled by 6233 *Duchess of Sutherland*. Seen at Elvetham in April 2007.

A welcome return to the main line was when Fastline resuscitated three Class 56s in 2006. In its handsome livery, 56303 speeds under the Met/GC overbridge near Kenton with a lengthy Birch Coppice to Grain intermodal service in July 2007.

Standard stock on the Waterloo to Reading lines is the Class 458 Juniper electric units. Passing Amen Corner, having just left Bracknell, set 8027 heads a pair on their way to Reading in August 2007.

Hull Trains replaced its Class 170s with Meridien Class 222s, one of which is seen on a down service from King's Cross to Hull, passing Hornsey in August 2007.

In January 2008, Hull Trains commenced operating a FO, SO and SuO service between King's Cross and Doncaster, using a DVT, five coaches and preserved Class 86 86101 *Sir William Stanier FRS*. The train is seen heading north through Brookmans Park in that month.

Passengers stand well back at Romford as Class 90 90005 speeds past on its way from Norwich to Liverpool Street in January 2008. The train carries the rather peculiar, but not unpleasant, One colours.

Two Class 67s were painted in Royal Claret colours, 67005 and 67006. The engines have often been used on special duties, as seen here at Magor in February 2008. 67006 *Royal Sovereign* speeds past with a Westbury to Cardiff Rugby football special.

In the original five-coach format, East Midlands Meridien Class 222 222013 speeds past Cossington in September 2008, whilst working from St Pancras to Derby. The Stagecoach colours blend nicely with the front end design.

In a rather different, smart South East Trains colour scheme, one of the ex-Merseyside EMUs Class 508 508203 leaves London Bridge for Tonbridge in November 2008, although to make the full journey in one of these sets would strain the body somewhat!

In the new corporate colours for the combined Yeoman and Hanson stone workings, Aggregate Industries Class 59 59001 *Yeoman Endeavour* rounds the bend at Crofton with the morning Merehead to Acton Jumbo service Taken in March 2009.

Northern Class 153 153360 stops at Hellifield with a Carlisle to Leeds service in July 2009. The decorative iron work of the platform canopy retains its charm.

Derived from the Class 332 Heathrow Express units, Northern Class 333 016 departs Guiseley with an Ilkley to Bradford service in July 2009. Note the old Midland Railway style diagonal fencing.

First Trans Pennine Class 185 185108, carrying various embellishments to do with events in Manchester, speeds through Mirfield with a Scarborough to Liverpool service in July 2009.

Fastline Class 66 66302 approaches Chesterfield in July 2009 with a matched set of loaded MGR bogie hoppers from Hatfield colliery to Ratcliffe power station. Taken in July 2009.

Very much off its normal beaten track, Wrexham & Shropshire, Class 67 67014 *Thomas Telford* passes Gospel Oak with a car train from Dagenham to Willesden in September 2009. The previous day it had been seen at Worting Junction with 66184 working from Hinksey to Eastleigh. Strange, to say the least!

With the motor luggage van almost resembling a locomotive, Class 460005 starts away from Gatwick Airport for Victoria in October 2009. Many of these units carried advertising liveries for related airlines serving Gatwick. The coaches have now been incorporated into SWT Class 458s.

Framed by the attractive footbridge at Maze Hill, South East Trains Class 465 465235 arrives with a Cannon Street to Dartford service in April 2010.

Engineering works on the North London line in the spring of 2010 meant freight diversions over the Tottenham & Hampstead Joint lines. So a nice surprise at Harringay Green Lane is a pair of DRS Class 57s, working the Tilbury to Daventry 'Sugarliner'. 57009 and 57004 are the locos, seen in April that year.

The layout at Norwood Junction, with Selhurst depot alongside, hosts Southern Class 377 377143 with a West Croydon to London Bridge train, while Class 171 171802 occupies the depot head shunt. A Class 455 stands in the station with a southbound train in April 2010.

Working from London Bridge to Uckfield in April 2010, Southern Turbostar Class 171 171727, a two-car unit, passes Penge West. The bridge in the background carries the down line from Sydenham to Crystal Palace.

Arriva Wales used some Class 57s when the business service between Holyhead and Cardiff first started (it now uses Class 67s). Passing Duffryn, 57313 is on the return working, in the plain colours used, although one loco, 57315, was fully decorated with Arriva lettering. The front end is marred by the Dellner coupling.

London Overground Class 378 378148 starts the descent from Haggerston to Dalston Junction with a train emanating from West Croydon in May 2010. At this time, Dalston Junction was the Northern terminus of the system. What a smart looking unit.

Parked amongst the buddleia at Cardiff in June 2010, Advenza Class 57 57005 shows off this short-term colour scheme, and hopes someone will purchase the loco. It subsequently went to West Coast Railways.

An Orpington to Charing Cross train leaves Petts Wood station in the hands of Electrostar unit Class 376 376024. The train carries the previous South East Trains livery. Taken in July 2010.

A few Class 321s were retained by the London Midland franchise when the Class 350s came on stream. In this view at Carpenders Park in August 2010, 321416 is working an early evening Euston to Tring commuter service.

The classic view from the bridge at Southall station shows a Siemens built Class 332 working a Heathrow Airport to Paddington express passing in August 2010. There was no chance of getting the unit number of this fast moving train.

South East Trains Class 375 375830 exits Rochester in September 2010, and heads for the tunnel before reaching Chatham. It is working a Victoria to Ramsgate/Dover service.

Some very pleasant views are to be had of HS1 in the Kent countryside, as seen here at Lenham Sidings, where a Class 395 Javelin streaks past on its way from Margate to St Pancras in September 2010.

Seen at track level rather than from the overbridge at Severn Tunnel Junction, Colas Class 66 66841 passes with a steel train from Llanwern to Dollands Moor in January 2011.

Carrying the Freightliner Heavy Haul colours introduced with the Class 70s, Class 90 90049 passes Armitage in April 2011 with a Felixstowe to Crewe intermodal service.

The race is on near Pinner where two Metropolitan line Class A units head towards Baker Street in April 2011. On the left is a train from Amersham, and on the right one from Watford.

The Bombardier Electrostar EMUs all look similar, but internal variations and colour schemes result in different class numbers. At Tottenham Hale, Class 379 379007 departs on its way from Liverpool Street to Stansted Airport in July 2011.

A nice surprise for the photographers at Cholsey was Arriva Wales blue Class 67 67003, passing with a Winchester to Southampton Pullman special on a glorious autumn day in October 2011. The train travelled via Salisbury, Westbury, Chippenham and Reading.

Trains pass at Headstone Lane in July 2012. Class 92 92016 *Brahms* now carries DB Schenker colours, and is working north with the Wembley to Daventry bottled-water train. Going the other way is a LOL Class 378 with a Watford Junction to Euston service.

In its unique *Flying Scotsman* purple colours, Class 91 91001 tails an express from Skipton to King's Cross, seen passing Welwyn Garden City in July 2012. A few Class 91s have carried non-standard colours at times.

On the same day at Welwyn Garden City, Grand Central Class 43 43480 heads an HST service from Sunderland to King's Cross. The striking colour scheme shows up well in the morning sun.

The year 2012 saw the use by Devon and Cornwall Railways of Class 56s carrying fly ash from the demolished Didcot power station to Calvert. On the return working with the empties, 56303 (an ex-Fastline loco) passes Hinksey in May of that year, leaving a cloud of fine particles behind it.

The most incredible sight at Winchfield in May 2013 was of the three Class 20s returning from Swanage to Clapham Junction. With two Transport for London decorated locos in the lead, 20189 and 20227, they were followed by blue 20142 and the preserved Class 423 4VEP 3417 *Gordon Pettitt*.

Very occasionally, First Great Western have decaled an HST power car in something other than the depressing First Group colours. An example was Class 43 43186 decorated for Hewlett Packard, seen tailing a Paddington to Swansea express passing Lower Basildon in May 2013, at a location now blighted by OHE masts.

National Rail adopted all-over yellow for its rolling stock. Illustrating this is the High Speed Measurement Train, headed by Class 43s 43062 with 43013 at the rear, passing Coedkernew in June 2013 whilst on a circuit from Old Oak common to Derby via Cardiff.

The Abellio Greater Anglia franchise adopted a basic white scheme for its trains. Passing the now-unobtainable location of Pudding Mill Lane in July 2013, Class 321 321448 is working from Liverpool Street to Southend. This unit has navy blue doors, but other Class 321s had red doors. One has to ask why?

A Goblin line Class 172 arrives at Gospel Oak from Barking. Class 172 172006 gingerly negotiates the points in August 2013.

Under a stormy sky in February 2014, Class 168 168219 leaves Banbury on its way from Birmingham Moor Street to Marylebone. The train carries the new Chiltern colours, and the scene is enhanced by the semaphore signals.

An afternoon Wembley Railnet to Shieldmuir working of three Class 325 units passes Headstone Lane in June 2014. The rear unit, 325003, carries a modified version of the original Royal Mail colours.

Some Virgin Pendolinos have also been decorated in various schemes over the years, some appalling such as the Graffiti version. Class 390 390155 carries X-Men vinyls and passes Carpenders Park in June 2014 with a Birmingham New Street to Euston express.

Although nicknamed 'Ugly Bettys' by some people, I personally do not find the Class 70s unattractive. Freightliner 70016 is seen in June 2014, passing through Tilehurst station on its way from Garston to Southampton MCT with an intermodal service.

In view of the previous statement, I have to qualify it by saying that I do not think the Colas colours suit a Class 70, whilst Freightliner green does. Passing Potbridge with the daily Eastleigh to Hoo Junction departmental, Colas 70809 is seen in June 2014 with a mixed consist of wagons.

There are less and less opportunities to see a Class 08 at work these days, so to see EWS 08799 doing its duty at Westbury in July 2014 was a nice bonus. It is also unusual to find one working with the radiator in front, rather than the cab.

The first of the Class 60s acquired by Colas passes Manor Farm, Cholsey with the Tilbury to Llanwern steel empties in September 2014. Trust a cloud to cross the train at a crucial moment!

The tanks running between Robeston and Theale have been rostered for a Class 60 for many years. The empties are seen passing Tilehurst in September 2014 behind DB Schenker liveried 60017.

In the new Great Northern colours, Class 365 365522 speeds through Welwyn Garden City with a Cambridge to Kings Cross service in October 2014.

The very smart new VTEC colours highlight this Edinburgh to King's Cross express, passing Alexandra Palace, propelled by Class 91 91124 in March 2015.

The Class 180s have now returned to their original hunting grounds on the Great Western lines. Passing Lower Basildon in March 2015, whilst there was a convenient gap in the masts, an unidentified set zooms past on its way from Paddington to Weston-super-Mare.

The latest class of locomotive to arrive in the UK is the Vossloh Class 68. In sparkling Chiltern grey and black, 68010 hurtles past South Ruislip in April 2015, on its way from Marylebone to Birmingham New Street.

Sometimes one can be caught unawares, such as on this occasion at Lower Basildon in April 2015, when preserved Deltic Class 55s D9000 *Royal Scots Grey* and 55019 *Royal Highland Fusilier* were returning from East Grinstead to Kidderminster, after a spell on the Bluebell Line.

Black Five 4-6-0 44871 has arrived at Mallaig with a load of satisfied passengers who have travelled from Fort William in June 1991.

Vesuvius erupts! 71000 *Duke of Gloucester* loses its feet completely as it approaches Didcot North Junction with a special working in April 1998. What the fireman thought when he surveyed the ruins of his fire is best left to the imagination!

Either the fireman has just put on a load of coal, or is not following LMS practice of firing, as BR standard 4-6-0 73096 lays down a smoke screen as it passes near Elvetham, with a Salisbury to Waterloo special in July 2003.

Merchant Navy Pacific 35028 *Clan Line* is a regular on the Surrey Hills steam specials. It is seen arriving at Shalford in January 2009 with an admiring audience.

In its first incarnation, Class A1 60163 *Tornado* hauled a Pathfinder special from Gloucester to Victoria in November 2009. It is seen at Sandhurst, a location very much off the normal trackage for steam workings.